Questions From the Prophet
Mowreh Elesha YisraEL

Questions on the Old Testament

ELesha YisraEL has formulated these 20 questions to prove beyond a shadow of a doubt that the Holy Scriptures or the so-called Old Testament is the Word of Our

Creator YAHWEH the Most High, and the other books: The New Testament and the

Quran are not the words of YAHWEH. He believes that if any serious student of the Scriptures attempts to honestly answer these questions that he/she would come to the same undeniable conclusion.

1. According to the Holy Scriptures (Old Testament), is it true that no man and I mean no man can die for another man's sin? **Deut 24:16, Ex. 33:33, Eze. 18:20-25**

2. According to the Holy Scriptures, is it true that the Kingdom of YAHWEH will be on this earth, and not in heaven

as the Christians teach? Gen. **17:7-8, Ex 6:6-8, Eze. 37:25-28**

3. According to the Holy Scriptures, is it true that the Pirst thing that YAHWEH will do when he returns to earth is to destroy everyone that will be eating the swine's Plesh (Hog) and the rat and the abomination? **Isa 66: 15-17**

4. According to the Holy Scriptures, is it true that the Most High condemns the Christmas tree? **Jer. 10:1-5**

5. **According to the Holy Scriptures, is it true that King David will be the King or (Messiah) that will rule the earth? Jer. 30:7-9, Eze. 34:22-24, Eze. 37: 21-28, Hos. 3:3-5, Isa. 55:3-5**

6. According to the Holy Scriptures, is it true that YAHWEH said YisraEL are his witnesses and they would witness

that there is no other God or Saviour besides him? **Isa 43:10-12, 21, Isa. 44:8**

7. **According to the Holy Scriptures, is it true that the Most High said sacriPices of animals are not necessary for the forgiveness of sin? Jer. 7:21, Ps. 40:6, Ps. 51:15-17, Micah 6:8, Hos. 6:6 I Sam. 15:22**

8. **According to the Holy Scriptures, is it true that the Creator, who made man in his own likeness and in his own image, has wooly hair? Dan. 7:9**

9. **According to the Holy Scriptures, is it true that the Almighty one of Jacob said in order to enter into the Kingdom every man must be circumcised in the Plesh and in the heart? Eze. 44:6-9**

10. According to the Holy Scriptures, is it true that white skin is a sign of sin? **Numbers 12:10-12, Deut. 24:8-9, II Kings 5:27, II Chron. 26:19-21**

11. According to the Holy Scriptures, is it true that worship of Jesus or anyone else is the greatest sin that could be committed? **Ex 32:30-35, Ex. 20:4-6, Deut. 30:15-20, Deut. 32:16-21, 30-43, Isa. 42:8**

12. According to the Holy Scriptures, is it True that YAHWEH made the Sabbath Day a sign between him and his people YisraEL forever? **Ex. 31:12-17, Eze. 20:12-20**

13. According to the Holy Scriptures, is it true that YAHWEH said his Laws, and Commandments should stand forever? **Deut. 30:19-20, Ecc. 3:14-15, Ecc. 12:12-14, Ps. 89:31, Ps 119:89, Ps. 119:52, Ps. 111:7-8, Isa/ 44:8, Isa 55:11, Mal. 3:6**

14. According to the Holy Scriptures, is it true that all of the Children of YisraEL were Black people with Woolly Hair and Most of

them wore their hair in Locks? **Ex. 4:4-7, Job. 30:30, Song of Sol. 1:5, Jer. 8:21, (Jer. 14:2, Ps 24:7), Lam. 4:8 Lam. 5:10, A description of their hair: Numb. 6:5, Judges 16:13, Song of Solomon 5:11, Eze. 44:20, This is the Most High: Dan. 7:9**

15. According to the Holy Scriptures, is it true that the only people that will inherit the Kingdom of YAHWEH (God) are those that keep his Commandments? **Ps. 1:1-6, Ps 37: 37-38**

16. According to the Holy Scriptures, is it true that although the New Testament and the Quran totally validates the Holy Scriptures (Old Testament). Contrary to this, the Torah completely condemns both books? **Deut. 4: 2, Deut. 12:32, Ecc. 3:14, Prov. 30: 5-6**

17. According to the Holy Scriptures, is it true that the Creator said the month of Abib (April) is the beginning of our months or the month that we should celebrate the New Year on, even though the blind carnal world

is doing otherwise. **Ex 12:1-2 Ex 13:4 Ex 34:18 Deut.16:1**

18. According to the Holy Scriptures that there were perfect men that walked this earth although the New Testament suggest otherwise. Noah, David I Kings 11:4 and 15:3 HezikiYAH II King 20:3-6 , Abraham Gen 17;1Asa, II Chron 15:17, Job 1:1-8, 2:**3**

19. Is it true that YAHWEH told his people, Children of YisraEL (So-called Negro) to never forget the laws and commandments he gave to Moses. Mal 4:4

20. Is it true that the Holy Scriptures or Torah (Old Testament) is the only book that has the holy days that YAHWEH gave to his people that are to be kept forever. Lev. 23:1-44

I Tim. 2:11, 12

Questions about the New Testament

ELesha YIsraEl has formulated these 20 questions to prove beyond a shadow of a doubt that the New Testament, is not the word of our Creator YAHWEH the Most High, but they are totally the opposite of the words of the Most High. He believes that if any serious student of the Scriptures attempts to honestly answer these questions that he/she would come to the same undeniable conclusion.

1. According to the New Testament, is it true that the Christ of the New Testament, gave the keys to the kingdom of heaven only to Peter? Matt. 16: 18-19. But thus saith YAHWEH is totally opposite: Ps. 50:6 Ps. 98:8-9

2. According to the New Testament, is it true that it is a shame for a woman

to speak in any of the Christian churches? I Cor. 14:33-35. But thus saith YAHWEH is totally opposite: **Jud. 4:4**

Judges 4:4,5

3. According to the New Testament, is it true that a woman can only be saved by bearing children? I Tim. 2:11-15. But thus saith YAHWEH is totally opposite: Gen. 1:28

4. According to the New Testament, is it true that the Christ of the New Testament, said he was not Elohim (God)? Was he lying? **John 20:7, Matt. 4:8-10, and 7:21, Rev. 3:12,** and look what YAHWEH said; Is. 43:10-12

5. According to the New Testament, is it true that the Christ of the New Testament, said that eternal life is when man knows the only true

Elohim (GOD)? John 17:3

6. According to the New Testament, is it true that Paul said he was stealing by taking or accepting money for preaching? II Cor. 11:7-8. Luke 10:1-4, 7 Thes. 2; 9 II Thes. 3:6-14. <u>But read what YAHWEH said; Mic. 3:11, Am. 9:7-15, 18.</u>

7. According to the New Testament, is it true that Jesus told a man that in order to be saved you had to keep all of Elohim's (GOD's) commandments? Matt. 19:16 but read what <u>YAHWEH said. Ecc. 12:12-13.</u>

8. According to the New Testament, is it true that Paul said that circumcision proPits nothing? I Cor. 7:19, Gal 5:2. But thus saith YAHWEH is totally opposite: Gen.

17:10-14, Ezek. 44: 6-9

9. According to the New Testament, is it true that Jesus said you would have to hate your father and mother, and sisters and brothers, and even hate yourself if you wanted to be a follower or disciple of his? Luke 14:25-26 **But thus saith YAHWEH is totally opposite: Ex. 20:12 Lev. 19:3, Deut. 27:16, Prov. 15:20**

10. According to the New Testament, is it true that Jesus did not even know the time or season that the fruit trees are suppose to bear fruit? **Mark 11:12-14. But thus saith YAHWEH is totally opposite: Prov. 28:5**

11. According to the New Testament, is it true that if one is a slave or a servant that he or she is to treat their master as if he were Christ? **Eph 6:5 But thus saith YAHWEH is totally opposite: Ex 4: 22-23**

12. According to the New Testament, is it true that leaders such as Mussolini, Adolph Hitler, and George W. Bush are considered servants of God and anyone that disobeys them are breaking the commandments of God; and will receive to themselves damnation? **Rom. 13:1-4. But thus saith YAHWEH is totally opposite: Dan. 6:13-26, Dan. 3:1-4,10-18**

13. According to the New Testament, is it true that Paul said if you have a daughter that is a virgin you should not allow her to marry until she is not able to have babies? **I Cor. 7; 34-37. But thus saith YAHWEH is totally opposite: Gen 1: 27-28, Ps. 127:3, Ps 128:3**

14. According to the New Testament, is it true that a Christian is not to owe anyone anything? **Rom 13:8, But thus saith YAHWEH is totally opposite: Deut. 15:11**

15. According to the New Testament, is it true that if a Christian is not married when he or she "comes to know Christ"; then, he or she is to remain unmarried? **I Cor. 7:27.**

But thus saith YAHWEH is totally opposite: Prov. 18:22

16. According to the New Testament, is it true that everybody in the kingdom of heaven will be impotent, and not able to have sex**? Matt. 22:28-29. But thus saith YAHWEH is totally opposite: Is. 60: 19-22 Ezek. 37: 22-24**

17. Is it true that Jesus called people workers of iniquity that are not keeping the Sabbath day and the other commandments of YAHWEH**? Matt. 7:21, and look what YAHWEH said: Deut. 30:15-20, Deut. 27:26, Deut. 28:1-68**

18. According to the New Testament,, is it true that Jesus said that anyone that worships him or anyone other than the father is false, and that the true worshipers should worship the father only, for the father seeketh such to worship him: **John 4:23, Also, YAHWEH said: Ps. 22:27, Ps 66:4, Zech. 14:16**

19. According to the New Testament,, is it true that anyone who attempts to obey the

laws and commandments of YAH, has fallen out of grace from Christ? **Gal. 5:2-4, But thus saith YAHWEH: Gen. 6:8-9, and Ps 84:11**

20. According to the New Testament, is it true that no man ever observed Sunday worship or Christmas, or Easter at anytime? And that the only days that a servant of the Most High shall observe are found in **Lev. 23:1-44?**

Questions about the Holy Quran

ELesha YIsraEl has formulated these 20 questions to prove beyond a shadow of a doubt that the Holy Quran is not the word of our Creator YAHWEH, but they are totally the opposite of the words of the Most High. He believes that if any serious student of the Scriptures attempts to honestly answer these questions that he/she would come to the same undeniable conclusion.

---

1. According to the Quran, is it true a Muslim man or woman can have sex outside of wedlock? **Surah 23: 1, 5-6 and 70: 29-31, But YAHWEH said: Deut 22:13-21, Deut 22:28-30**

2. According to the Quran, is it true that a Muslim can Prostitute a woman? **Surah 24:32-33, But YAHWEH said: Lev. 19:29, Numb. 15:15-16**

3. **According to the Quran is it true that a Muslim can beat his wife? Surah 4: 34. But YAHWEH said: Gen. 2:22-24, Lev. 19:17, Prov. 25:24**

4. According to the Quran is it true that there is no law against raping a woman, or aborting a baby? **Ex. 21:22-27 Deut. 22:25-26**

5. According to the Quran is it true that only people with white faces will be granted permission into Paradise and people with black faces will be turned away? **Surah 3: 105-108, 28:32, But YAHWEH said: Numb. 12:4-12, Deut. 24:8-9, II Kings 5:27**

6. According to the Quran is it true that the angel Gabriel told Muhammad after giving him the revelation of the Quran, that if he has any questions go to those who had been reading the book before him. (Speaking of the Children of YisraEL) Surah 10:94, 26:192-197, 40:53-54, 29:27, 32:23, 6: 89-90. But YAHWEH said. Ps 147:19-20

7. According to the Quran is it true a Muslim can eat Rats, dogs, and any animal except a Pig. But they can eat a Pig if they are really hungry? Surah 5:3-4, 6:145, 6:118-119. But YAHWEH said Lev. 11:14-8, Deut. 14:1-20

8. According to the Quran is it true that a Muslim is breaking the law of Allah, if they refuse to eat cats, dogs, and rats? Surah 2:172-173, 5:87-88, 6:118-119 6:145:146, But YAHWEH

said Lev:20:24-26

9. According to the Quran is it true that worshiping Jesus or anyone other than Allah, is a sin that one can never be forgiven for? **Surah 4:48**

10. According to the Quran is it true that the Holy Quran is supposed to be the Torah or the Laws of the so-called Old Testament written in the Arabic language? **Surah 46:12, 10:94, 40:53**

11. According to the Quran is it that Allah hates the deaf and the dumb? **Surah 8; 20-22, 2:18-20, But YAHWEH Said Isa. 35:1-6**

12. According to the Quran is it true that the Quran said the sun sets down every night in the murky pond? **Surah 18:86, But YAHWEH said Gen. 1:14**

13. **According to the Quran is it true that the Children of YIsraEl was told they were not to eat dogs and rats and other animals with claws, or the fat on animals because of our disobedience? Surah 6:146 But YAHWEH said Lev. 11-1-4**

14. According to the Quran is it true that the slave is never to be made equal to his owner? **Surah 16:17**

15. According to the Quran is it true a woman can desert her husband? **Surah 60:10 But YAHWEH said Gen. Ex 20:14, Deut. 22:22 Lev. 18:20, Gen. 39:7-9**

16. According to the Quran is it true a Muslim should even fight his own brother if he does not believe in Allah nor follow the religion of truth? **Surah 9:29, But YAHWEH said Lev. 19:17-18**

17. According to the Quran is it true that earth was made in six days; **Surah 7:45,**

10:3 or was it eight days? 41:9-10, But YAHWEH Said Gen 2: 1-2, Ex. 20:8-11

18. According to the Quran is it true that Mary is the Mother of Jesus; **Surah 3:47,** or was he made from the dust of the earth like Adam? **Surah 3:59:60**

19. According to the Quran is it true that a Muslim should not take Christians for friends, because they will loose favor with Allah**? Surah 5:51** Or is it true that Christians are the closest and nearest of friends to a Muslim? **Surah 5:82**, Prov. 11:1

20. According to the Quran, is it true that in the Muslim paradise, or heaven that the males will have sex slaves that will be confined to tents. **Surah 55: 60-72**.

Questions on Who is YisraEL?

ELesha YisraEL has formulated these 15 questions to prove beyond a shadow of a doubt, that YisraEL is and always have been a black nation. He believes that if any serious student of the scriptures who attempts to answer these questions will come to the same undeniable conclusion that YisraEL is a Black nation and part of that nation is the Black Man in America.

1. Is it true that the House of YisraEL is a Black nation? Jer. 14:1-2. Ps 24:7-8, Jer. 8:21, Job 30:30

2. Is it true that the Children of YisraEL's prophets were described as being Black? Ex 4:1-8, Song of Solomon 1:5

3. Is it true that the Children of YisraEL's Nazerites were blacker that coal? Lam. 4:7-8, Lam5:10

4. Is it true that if the YisraELites were black then they would always remain black? Jer. 13:23

5. Is it true that the children of YisraEL had wooly hair? Song of Solomon 5:11

6. Is it true that many of the Children of YisraEl wore locks? Num. 6:5 Judges 16:3, Song of Solomon 5:11 Eze. 44:21

7. Is it true that YAHWEH, who is the Creator of the Heaven, the Sea, and the Earth, had Wooly Hair? Dan. 7:9

8. Is it true that the Children of YisraEL were to go into slavery for 400 years? Gen. 15:13-14

9. Is it True that the Children of YisraEL are the only people in the world that were taken out of their land as a result of slaver and have never returned to their home until this day?
   Deut. 28:68, Hos. 3:4-5, Ps. 83:1-5

10. Is it true that the Enemies of YAHWEH'S people would take them out of their land in ships, were they were to remain until YAHWEH redeems them in the last day? Deut. **28:68**

11. Is it true that the House of YisraEL was to have their family broke up and sold and their wives were to be raped? Deut. **28:36-44**

12. Is it true that the Children of YisraEL were to look like a speckled

bird, as a result of their wives being raped? Jer. 12:9

13. Is it true that the Enemies of YAHWEH'S people who also hated him would change our name so we could not function as a nation? Ps 83:1-4

14. Is it True that YAHWEH said all of the other nations would hate us, because we rejected our true Elohim (God)? Jer. 12:9, Deut. 28:45-50

15. Is it true that we the Children of YisraEL was to be called Proverbs, Bywords, such as nigger, negro, jigga boos, porch monkeys, and vagabonds because of our disobedience.?
Deut. 2

Questions on Jesus

ELesha YisraEL has formulated these questions to prove beyond a shadow of a doubt that the elect seed of YisraEL is the one that YAHWEH loves more than anything on

this Earth and not Jesus as we have been taught. He believes that if any serious student of the scriptures attempts to answer these questions, that they would come to the same undeniable conclusion.

1. According to the Holy Scriptures (Old Testament) who did YAHWEH say was his "First Born Son," YisraEL or Jesus? Ex. 4:22:23, Hos. 11: 1

2. Who did the Most High say he would raise from the grave in 3 days, YisraEL or Jesus? Hos. 6:1-2

3. Who did the Almighty say was the "Apple of his Eye," YisraEl or Jesus? Zec. 2:7-8, Deut. 323:10

4. Who did YAHWEH say he was married to, and was his "Bride," YisraEL or Jesus? Jer. 3:14, Isa 62:5 Hos. 2:19-21

5. Who did YAHWEH say would be brought to him for an offering in a "Clean Vessel," (Body) YisraEL or Jesus? Isa. 66:20

6. Who did the Most High say he would be his battle axe, and his "weapon of war.," YisraEL or Jesus? Jer. 51:19-20

7. Who did YAHWEH say that he would give for a "Light," to the Gentiles, YisraEL or Jesus? Isa

42:6-24, Isa. 49:1-6, 60:3

8. Who did YAHWEH propose to give to the world for a "Covenant," YisraEL or Jesus? Isa. 42:6-24 Isa. 49:3-7-8

9. Who did the Creator say would be with him until the End of Time, YisraEL or Jesus? Isa 45:17, Eze. 37:24-28

10. Who did YAHWEH say his **"Glory,"** would be seen upon, YisraEL or Jesus? **Isa. 60:1-3 Isa. 35:2, Isa. 43:7, Isa. 46:13, Isa. 66: 18**

11. Who did YAHWEH say he formed and Created for the purpose of **Praising him,** YisraEL or Jesus? **Isa. 43:21**

12. Who did YAHWEH say he called from the womb, and made mention of his name, while he was still in the Bowels of his

mother and made his mouth like a sharp sword and said through Thee shall I be **Glorihied,** YisraEL or Jesus? **Isa 49:1-7**

13. Who did YAHWEH say was the " **Everlasting Gates,"** for whom He the King of Glory would come in, YisraEL or Jesus? **Ps 24:6-10**

14. Who did YAHWEH refer to **"The dearly beloved of is soul,"** was it YisraEL or Jesus? **Jer. 12:7, Deut. 33:12**

15. What was the name of the person that was never spoken of out of the mouth of YAHWEH? Was it Jesus? Yes, it was...

If it is true that this there is no name under Heaven whereby man can be saved other than Jesus, and in fact if Jesus Is the son of Elohim (God) and the most important person in the bible and indeed the world. Than my question is, why is it that his name is not mentioned at all by anyone in the Holy Scriptures (Old Testament)?

May YAH Bless You. ELesha YisraEL

Day & Night Questions

ELesha YisraEl has formulated these 21 questions to prove beyond a shadow of a doubt that a day starts in the morning, and ends in the evening; and evening is a part of a day, and not the beginning of a new day. He believes that if any serious student of the Scriptures attempts to honestly answer these questions that he would come to the same undeniable conclusion that day

and night are totally the opposite of one another, and there two distinctly different times altogether.

1. According to **Gen. 1:14**, what did **YAH**, Our Creator, give us to determine our **days** and our years. (Q) **Lights** or **darkness (nights)?**
(A) - **Lights. Gen. 1:14, notice not darkness (nights), but "lights".**

2. If a day starts in the evening when it becomes dark, then when does a night begin?

(A) - They do not both start simultaneously, if so, they would be the same. A day starts when it becomes light Judges 16:2, and a night starts when it becomes dark (Psalm 104:20). They are totally the opposite of one another. Gen. 8:22.

3. At 12:00 **midnight**, is that the **middle of the night** or the **middle of the day**?
(A) - It is the middle of the night, because the middle of the day comes after the morning and before the evening. **I Kings 18:26-29.**

4. When the Holy Scriptures speak about the **break of day**, or the **dawning of the day** in **2 Samuel 2:32, Judges 19:25 and Job 7:4;**

(Q) Is this speaking about the **beginning of a day**, or the **ending of a day**? **(A)** - It is speaking about the beginning of a day.

5. Was the sun made to rule over the day or was it made to **rule over the night?** (See **Gen. 1:14-18 and Psalms 136:7-9**).If

the **sun** was made to **rule over the day**, then how

can a **day** begin at **night** when the **sun** is not ruling? (A) - Totally impossible. **Psalm 136:7-9**.

6. The Creator said many times throughout the Scriptures, **(Gen. 1:3-4 and Gen. 1:14-18)** that He divided the **day** from the **night** or the **light** from **darkness**.

(Q) - When did He put them back together? (A) - Never! **Ecclesiastes 3:14 and Isa. 40:8.**

7. Is it possible for my son to remain at your house all day without spending the **night**? (A) - Yes, because when a day ends, the night begins. **Psalm 104:20.**

8. In **Numbers 11:32**, it says that the Children of YisraEl gathered the quails all that **day**, and all that **night**, and all the next **day**.

(Q) - How many **days** and how many **nights** did they gather quails?

(A) - Two **days** and one **night**, (but if a **day** begins at **night** then they would have gathered quails three **days** and three **nights**).

9. According to **Lev. 8:35**, Aaron and his sons were to remain at the door of the Tabernacle, **day** and **night**, seven **days**. (Q) How many **nights** did they remain?

(A) - Six **nights**.

10. In **Lev. 7:15**, it says, "the flesh of the sacrifice of His peace offerings for thanksgiving shall be eaten the same **day** that it is offered; he shall not leave any of it until the **morning**." (Q) Does the word "**morning**," in this verse indicate the **morning** that is connected to the previous **evening**, or the **morning** that is connected to a new **day**? (A) - New **day**. **Num. 28:3-4**, this verse also proves the **evening** is part of the previous **day**, not the beginning of a new **day**.

11. In **Exodus 18:13** it states, and it came to pass on the **morrow**, that Moses sat to judge the people: and the people stood by Moses

from the **morning** unto the **evening**.
(Q) When does **morrow** begin; in the **evening**, **night** or in the **morning**?
(A) Morning, as all of the Scriptures clearly indicates. I have never found a Scripture where the **morrow** starts in the **evening** or the **night**.

12. According to **Exodus 16:22-25**, when does the **Rest of the Holy Sabbath** unto **YAH** begin, in the **night**, **evening** or in the **morning**?

(A) Morning or **morrow**, as all new **days** begins.

13. If a **night** is considered a **day**, then what did **YAH** mean when He said that He caused it to rain forty **days** and forty **nights**?

(A) - A **night** is not considered a **day**. **Psalm 104:20**.

14. If a **day** starts when it becomes **dark**, then why is **darkness** always pertained to as **night**, and never pertained to as **day**? **(Psalm 104:20)**; except when it is speaking

about the "**Day** of **YAH's** Wrath."**?** (**A**) A **day** does not start when it becomes **dark**, because **YAH** totally separated the light from the darkness. **Gen. 1:18**.

15. In **Gen. 1:5**, does the word day mean light or does it mean light and darkness? (**A**) The word **day** means **light** only. **Gen. 1:3-4**.

16. **Gen. 8:22** reads, "While the earth remaineth, seedtime and harvest, and cold and heat, and summer and winter, and **day and night** shall not cease." **The Most High** gives us four different times and conditions. (**Q**) Are these times and conditions the same, or are they totally the opposite of one another? (**A**) Totally the opposite of one another.

17. In **Job 17:8-12**, why is it that the upright men, the innocent men, and the righteous men and everyone who has clean hands has stirred up themselves against the hypocrites? (**Q-a**) Why is it that the people who changed **night into day** are referred to as hypocrites?

(A) Because the hypocrites are saying that **YAH**, Our Creator told a lie, when He said He separated the **day** from the **night**. **Gen. 1:14-18**.

(Q-b) If a **day** always started at **night**, then how could anyone change the **night** into **day**? **(A)** Totally impossible, but by the wicked trying to do so, it could possibly bring about the **total destruction** of the **House of YisraEl**. **Jer. 33:19-21**.

18. According to the Words of **The Most High**, what is the difference between a **day** and a **night**? (Give Scriptures please).

(A) Day equals **light**, and darkness equals **night**. **Jer. 31:35 and Psalm 136:7-9**.

19. In **Jer. 33:19-21, YAH** speaks about the evil that He would bring upon the house of David and kingdom of YisraEl, if they broke His covenants that there should not be **day or night in their season (Psalm 22:2).** **(Q)** What is the **season of the day**, and what is the **season of the night?** **(A)** The sun is the **season of the day (Gen. 1: 1:16-18)**,

and the moon is the **season of the night Jer. 31:35.**

20. Outside of the way that many of you might interpret **Genesis 1st Chapter**, is there anywhere else in the Holy Scriptures that says that **evening and morning are a day?** (**A**) No! Because, it is not, neither is **Genesis 1st Chapter** saying that.

21. If the celebration of our Sabbath days and our new moons (**Isa. 66:23**) begins in the **evening** when the **sun is going down**, why would Our Creator state that all nations shall praise His Name and worship Him from the "**rising of the sun until the going down of the same (sun)?**" (**A**) If the Sabbath started in the **evening**, as many of our people believe, then these verses would make no sense whatsoever. **Malachi 1:11** reads, "For **from the rising of the sun** even unto the going down of the same, My Name shall be Great among the Gentiles, and in every place **incense shall be offered unto My name, and a pure offering**: for My Name shall be Great among the heathen, saith

YAH of Hosts." **Psalm 113:3 and Psalm 50:1.**

QUESTIONS ON THE SABBATH

ELesha YisraEL has formulated these 15 questions to prove beyond a shadow of a doubt that we, the Sons and Daughters of YAHWEH, should only observe the seventh day of the week (Saturday), as our Holy Sabbath Day. He believes that if any serious student of the Scriptures

attempts to honestly answer these questions that he/she would come to the same undeniable conclusion.

1) According to the word of **YAH,** who does the Sabbath belong to? **A - Genesis 2:1-3 Exodus 16:23-25 and Exodus 20:10**

2) What day of the week did **YAH,** Our Creator **Bless, Hallow and Sanctify the first day or the seventh day?**
A - Genesis 2:3 and Exodus 20:11

3) What day did **YAH** our Creator would be a sign between Him and His people **forever?**
A - Exodus 31:12-17 and EzekiEl 20:12

4) What time of day did **YAH** start His seventh day Sabbath? **A - Exodus 16:23-25**

5) What day did The Most High include within the Ten Commandments which He wrote with His finger on a tablet of stone, the first day (Sunday), or the seventh day(Saturday)? **A - Exodus 20:8-11 and Deuteronomy 5:6-14**

6) Was the Sabbath Day made for man or was man made for the Sabbath?

A - Leviticus 23:3 and EzekiEl 20:12

7) Did the Christ of the New Testament keep **YAH's** seventh day Sabbath? **A - Matthew 5:17-19**

8) What day did JC's and his disciples worship on the first day or the seventh day?

A - Acts 13:13-14, Acts 17:2, and Acts 18:4

9) What day of week did the Gentiles who alleged received grace, worship on?

A - Acts 13:42-44

10) Were the disciples of JC ever commanded to keep the 1st day (Sunday), as a day of worship?

A - No. Matthew 23:1-3

11) Is there anywhere in the entire Bible where it says that, every day is holy?

A - No! Proverbs 30:5-6

12) Will the Sabbath Day still be kept in the New Kingdom?

A - Yes. Isaiah 66:22-24

13) What day did Our Creator attach a **curse** to, and said if we would not observe this day, that we would be separated from His people forever, the 1st day Sunday or the **seventh day (Saturday)?**
A - Exodus 31:12-14

14) Did the Christ of the New Testament, or any of his disciples, ever give any of their followers, another **Sabbath Day** other than the seventh day of the week?
A - Matt 5:17-19

15) Who did the Holy Scriptures say is "**Our Only Judge, Our Only King, and Our Only Lawgiver**"?
A - Isaiah 33:22

Questions on The Passover

ELesha YisraEL has formulated these 12 questions to prove beyond a shadow of a doubt that we should not keep the Passover, Feast of Unleavened Bread, Feast of Weeks, nor the

Feast of Tabernacles, anywhere outside of Jerusalem. Any one that does so is seriously violating the commandments of YAH, Our Creator. See Deuteronomy 27:26.

1. Is one violating the Law of **YAH** by attempting to celebrate the Passover outside of the holy land?
    a. Yes. Exodus 12:23-25, Deuteronomy 16:5-6 also verse 16.

2. Can any male that is not **born** in the house of a **YisraELite** or **brought** with his money **keep the Passover?**
    a. No. Exodus 12:43-45 & 48-49

3. Where is the place that **YAH** has chosen to place His name at? **a. II Chronicles 6:5-6, and II Chronicles 33:4**

4. How many **Passovers** are there in one year? **a. Two, Numbers 9:9-11**

5. Did the Children of YisraEL ever celebrate the **Passover** in the land of their captivity? **a. No. Ezra 6:16-18**

Look

6. If an YisraELite is unable to celebrate the **Passover**, must they still remove all the leaven out of their houses? **a. Yes, Exodus 12:20, Exodus 13:7, and Deuteronomy 16:4**

7. If we were in the **Promised Land**, could we celebrate the **Passover** within any of our **gates**?

a. No. **Deuteronomy 16:5-6 and Deuteronomy 16:16**

8. According to the Word of **YAH**, if a person is not **circumcised** are they allowed to keep the **Passover**?
   a. No. Exodus 12:43-48

9. Can anyone that worships Jesus in any way, allowed to keep **YAH'S** Holy Feast Days?
   a. No. Deuteronomy 13:1-6, Deuteronomy 30:15-20 and John 4:22-23.

10. How many complete days are the **Passover** and the **Feast of Unleavened bread**?

a. Seven days. Leviticus 23 :5-8 " In the fourteenth day of the first month at

even is **YAH'S Passover. 6) And on the fifteenth day of the same month is the Feast of Unleavened bread unto YAH: seven days ye must eat unleavened bread. 7) In the first day ye shall have a holy convocation: ye shall do no servile work therein. 8) But ye shall offer an offering made by fire unto YAH seven days in the seventh day is a holy convocation ye shall do no servile work therein."**

11. Are we allowed to celebrate the **Feast of Unleavened Bread, the Feast of Weeks, and the Feast of Tabernacles**, any place other than where we kept the **Passover** at?

a. No. Deuteronomy 16:5-6 and Deuteronomy 16:16

12. Can one be a **true** servant of **YAH** and still celebrate the **Passover outside** of **Jerusalem**?

a. No. Deuteronomy 4:2 and Proverbs 30:5-6

Jeremiah 23:21-22, "I have not sent these prophets yet they ran ; I have not spoken to them, yet they prophesied. But if they had stood in my counsel, and had caused my people to hear my words, then they should have turned them from their evil way and from the evil of their doings."

Isaiah 8:20 "To the Law and to the Testimony; if they speak not according to this Word, it is because there is no light in them."

Questions on the Passover And Feast of Unleavened Bread Pertaining to Day and Night

Elesha YisraEL has formulated these 10 questions to prove beyond a shadow of a doubt that we the Children of YisraEL, did not come out of Egypt on the night of the Passover. He believes that if any serious student of the scriptures attempts to honestly answer these

questions that he/she would come to the same undeniable conclusion that the 46

1. What day and time did the Passover start?

a. Exodus 12:6, and Leviticus 23:5

2. What day and what time did Passover End?

a. Exodus 12:12 and Exodus 12:29

3. What time did the actual Passover occur?

a. Exodus 12:12 and Exodus 12:29

4. What day and what time did the Feast of Unleavened Bread start?

a. Leviticus 23:6 and Numbers 28:17

5. What day and what time did the Feast of Unleavened Bread end?

a. Exodus 12:18, and Leviticus 23:8

6. Did we celebrate the Passover the same night we came out of Egypt?

a. No, Numbers 33:3

7. Does the 14th day at even represent the beginning of a day or the end of a day?

a. End of a Day, Deut. 16:6 Leviticus 23:32

8. When did YAHWEH pass over the houses of the Children of YisraEL, was it the night of the 14th or the night of the 15th?

a. II Chronicles 35:14-16, also Exodus 12:8-12

9. What night was to be a memorial, the night of the 14th or the night of the 15th?

a. Exodus 12:14 and Exodus 12:42

10. What is the main significance of the Feast of Unleavened Bread?

a. Exodus 12:17 and Exodus 12:42

© 2014 World Ingathering of the Children of YisraEL

For More Information: Go to

House of YisraEL of Cincinnati

www.worldgatheringyisrael.org

1907 Vine St. Cincinnati, OH 45202

Moreh IshiYAH YisraEL

(919)931-6216

Moreh IshYAH YisraEL

(513)237-5911

Moreh Naphtali YisraEL

(513) 374-9902